Parting After Parting

Parting After Parting

A collection of new poems by Jang Seok-won
Translated by Deborah Kim

K POET

아시아

Contents

PARTING AFTER PARTING

This is an erased chronicle on endemic disease

When did that vanishing cloud come into being

Tanzania made a leopard out of me

Joy makes me cry out

At the sight of a zebra
Suddenly
I sprout fangs

I tread forgetting fear

I move with hunger without false steps

Like the wind before my birth I am eternally returning

Invincible

Mane of hair pulled into wind
Sunlight—cliffs—fissures
Move

From earth to horizon
Like the loping wolf

Green, luminous gong
Rings out—hit the gong—ring ring
Its green heart bursts

Green confronts sky and stomach
Each sticks to the other

Sand flows into eye sockets

*

Seems life and death are unknowable here

The sound of a warrior's breath wreaking havoc from end to end

The hatred of dust

Flares retrace their paths and burn back down to their roots

I watch them die out

Spring, screaming

From the
Bed
From the
Table

To the moment
The bottle of pills falls

Another face arrives
I melt under
That other face

It's a child ruptured
It's a child trapped

Submerged
You don't know how to cry

You pierce the skin and emerge
You, all sharpness
Spring leaping forward on one leg

The children have left

Green
Drill
Shepherd's Purse
Abdomen
Excavation in Progress

Daddy cool

I puff up like a pale ball
After I'm popped sparks will fly
A pigeon flaps its wings
It's docile—it takes after me
If you want I can be even more obedient

Think about an expanding universe
Do you live there
Then I'll be ruined
Am I growing closer to you
Then I'll be happy

Willing to, gladly, adjust orbit

Inner walls grow damp
After the voice breaks
Blood flows harder
Rears like a bull
Grows violent like a bull

How will my life end
Destruction in the blink of an eye
How could I be so obsessed with only you?
Adios, Adidas, Adonis

How could you pour all that love into me?

I want to be cyborgized like Mechander Robo

Push hunks of meat deep into me
Dismantle me down to my proteins

Prism

How could that happen
How could a love like that
Begin

Shadows flicker outside the window
Dark cold and gaunt

The skies are clearing but we

We will stuff each other's bodies at night
We'll sniff sniff at each other
We'll slice and gnaw at red flesh to digest each other

Light spilling out between splintered bone

Summer solstice

Some silences in fact

You turn me into skin and bones
Shadows crawl—grow longer

To remember your languid yawn

A faint breeze

Inside a car racing on the beltway in broad daylight
Though you might murmur about being lonely
The moment you remember me

I open my mouth to swallow you whole
You run far away to forget me

Vivid foul breath

Mutant

I fall prey to
An attack of history

Admit defeat

Even when I smile my teeth don't show
I want to sing even if I sing only carols

I sit on the toilet reading Korea
After General Park's death
History has become dough to be kneaded

1979, history, material nouns

Fireworks, democracy

In the midst of chaos reality is desperate
Love is a derangement—your momentary delusion
The future is white blood cells teeming with failure
All of us are tired

There's a crowd like never before in the square
I'm having fun like a crowned beauty pageant queen
And public order in the streets
Is euphoric—the pleasure of being injected

with tranquilizer

I am vigorously transforming

Superman returns

A firebomb flies from left to right
Catapulted by the White Skull Brigade
A precise and persistent severance

Only grey souls remember the yearning
Utopia is fiction—Our ideologies were
Lies—In that moment the Southpaw sniper stood alone
Covered in tear gas powder

The illusions I wove
The work clothes smeared with blood
Were of course unveiled as pure baseless fantasy

The only constant, love
A pure creed that worked
To nourish and feed me
Formless, love ruled me

Red the empire and the general's blood

The stars whisper above the streets of Hong Kong at night…
If you buy this body that struggles as it learns
Surely it will become ... a revolutionary machine

There was a platform of labor liberation and

driving out American imperialism

  It's a miracle, baby

Hero

A crow with a stick in its beak flies to the peak
The end of progress
When delusional loneliness was destroyed

No one betrayed their country
Beauty was made real

You use me to proselytize
I consume myself ardently for you

I expose my scars and am transformed
If you shave away at your body in order to disappear
We'll wallow in relief

There was nothing that could be done
To change the world
(Martyrdom for the future—an alliance in the face of loneliness)
Struggle and ideology and labor unions are dead languages

Towards an impossible happiness
I'll be the Monkey King Sun Wukong
I soar
(Flying Nimbus!)

O long ennui O brief terror

The world grows even crueler

We play master and servant together

Under construction

How thin will we grow

Can a split rock grow whole again

I wish I could save even just one person…

Banners and flyers are trampled
The Taegeukgi parades grow closer

There was never a time that my fate was changed by love

Now
A time for roaming

Resurrected people
Starving dogs
Looking to shred flesh

As much as I loved you
As much as I was loved
If I were to love you again
I'd bash a rock against my head

You construct me

I slaughter myself

Pointillism

What to do after being conquered
Commands—overwhelming—smooth—like
night's velvet—dense—
The world's pressure points

Into the jaws of smoke
Into the thorax of darkness

You left because I wasn't enough
You're beyond infinite velocity
Melting down—slipping
. . . .

Lack of love damaged us both

Lack of love broke us both

Unfurling to bloom
Your body and mine

Flowers, buried alive
Flowers, burning alive

Hyperreality

A magpie
Flies
Between my eyes

I'm squid-ing
But my friend
Erases me

My face outside
Circles triangles
Grows faint

It's an afternoon where
Cephalopods feed on

Playground kids

Assembled
Sunbeams

August
Someone touches me
I roast red

I go
Inward
Disappear deep
Into the squid

Zipper mouth

You threw me away

I cry crumple-mouthed

Nexus

I found you again

You fled at my touch

Lovers hang from cocoons

The gnawing wind the thinning skin

The butterfly crushed before its wings can even dry

Flux

One drop
Of blood

Like a burst
Water balloon

Within a
Shredded silence

You are in
A state of mitosis

Eternity

On the local bus the child silently clasps his hands

A leaf falls and sticks to his thigh like a tentacle's sucker

I walk holding my young father's hand

At the end of the road we'll part ways

The day we meet again

The gap grows wider
The road faces west

Green trees line the road
Green screams spill out

It's not too late
No, it's already over

It's possible to go back
Sure, it's impossible to go back

It's clear the two of us
Can't see anything

Skin cracks

Grows apart spreads apart

I watch you and wait

Take me back

The lesser of two evils

There was no reply

Trees line the road like sentries

Drawn into summer

It feels like I'm walking

In your chest

Deep into your being
Inside, to a hotter place

Once we reach Goksan
You'll disappear

I was alone
Then we became each other

Left alone
Until the last

I'll walk
Until I rot away

Cheers, my darkness, cheers

Kyrie eleison

Speechless and unconscious
I lose you I erase myself

I stand naked in front of the mirror
You gaze at me
You pull at my body

Droplets of water take shape
Draw close to me
I am full of flame

White light dawns

There was a rupture

Breath, traces of your existence

You were tender
A body grateful

*

Children play on twin graves
You place a hand on my body
The dead surround us
One darkness another darkness
Surround us, surround us again
One sip another sip
I breathe in your breath

You become clear
Your face in stark relief in the void

Risen on a Black Sabbath
Your body is here
Hazy heart to hazy heart

The things that try to disappear
The things that try to return
Get tangled grow soggy

A sea of black blood in the old tree

I lost you I threw you away

I am wasting away skin and bones
A just punishment for my crimes against love

Bright blue eyes shine
A beast bites the scruff

You've returned

Will o' the wisp float between burial mounds
You take me there we lie down together

Into the warm body of darkness
I soothe you
Stars flicker above your forehead

Lofty deep persistent love
Incarnate

The Angles of a Wreckage

The August light
Shatters the shadows

Goodbyes
Truly
Are beautiful

Hot plants
Spread out

Somewhere nearby

The promise

Of the countless milkweeds

To return
Has been fulfilled

Once more

Entwined
Close relations
Come into being

Bone Fracture

Discarded and broken

The air is full of

Tears shed blood shed

I've caressed you for thirty years
What did I do wrong

A single phrase I love you

Each word

Bent and broken

Limped away only to pause

Look back

I burn

POET'S NOTE

Poetry needs change. It needs movement. I want to change language. I reject the language of today, the language of servitude, of treachery. It is impossible to rehabilitate the body. I want to metamorphose into a new body of language and reject "their" language. I believe in the possibility of this. Its body heat and its musk are distinct. Without transformed sentence structure and form, language and the body cannot be changed. Impossibility and possibility coexist. The languages of the world need to be transformed—the languages of power and ideology and injustice. I dream of a language revolution, the arrival of a language movement with an unexpectedly perpetual engine.

I want to know the predicate of the sentence where "language" is the subject. What is language?

POET'S ESSAY

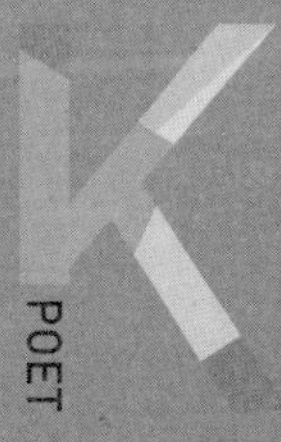

A third love will come to me. Fate will take me. You break my heart. (I think it's a lie. It turned out to be false without evidence.) So, this is life (i.e. imaginary). Apartments can be seen beyond the monitor (modernity). I am writing beneath the gray western skies, but I don't think of this as writing. Without you, nothing can be love. The language (reality) that passes through my body, it is the beginning and the end. The creation and destruction of poetry. What moves, moves toward eternity.

Writing "you" doesn't make you appear. Poetry is nothing.

What thought, what feeling, what emotion should be mobilized (trained) for me to write a single paragraph (sentence)? After being used what (who) will fill that empty space? Who will (what will) return under the blue skies? A convulsion (a red autumn) will come (eventually, something). I look out the window and with music by my side, gaze at blue skies and sink into dreams. The heart moves the body (you move me). Will we be able to finish parting before tomorrow comes? Each day is long and prolonged. (Sewn and mended.) No work (no you) is freedom. I exalt you. I don't mind who (or what) I may become. You used to be everything, but now you've become something, and I've become that. We are nothing but melancholy things. We abandoned each other and were abandoned.

"You" have become a non-person subject.

The smell of Chapaguri envelops the entire house. A child is eating at a wooden table softly blowing on the noodles. Orange LED light. The sound of rain over the stopped music. Your olfactory hallucination. As long as you live, sadness will not vanish. As long as you live, love will never be (not the first love nor the second). We have no choice but to deceive and be deceived, holding onto one last hope (each other). There is no end in sight. There comes a time when you want to give up everything. The trees will be gone (ablaze). We will be drawn into winter (the mirror). Don't call it a parting. You were a dream. Life is a simulation symbols.

It's a beautiful life!

I ask, is it possible to love and be loved? (I

bury this question.) I can't go back; I can't come back. Changing from cold-hearted (warm-hearted) to heartfelt (heartless), at parting after parting.

Darknesss falls. I ask if there's someone I (do not) miss. Who am I to answer that there are many? Even oblivion is warming up. Music surrounds me without pause. You're disappearing. Where are you going (my second, my first loves)? How did I get here? Stop.

COMMENTARY

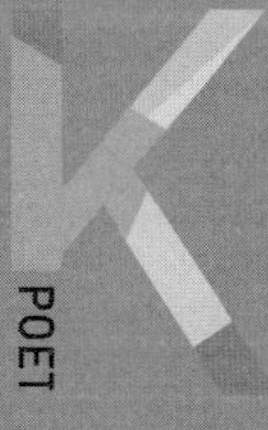

O! O, happy heart! Yes, joyful life!

Park Sang-su (Poet, Literary critic)

It has been more than ten years since I first met Jang Seok-won. As my senior in the literary world, while I cannot claim a special connection to him, we have spent time together over the years socializing with colleagues over drinks or attending talks hosted by literary magazines. The impression he left on me was that of an approachable writer who didn't lord his seniority over others. He enjoys a good joke and, above all else, he is fond of spending time with people. In any social setting, Jang Seok-won stands out due to his cheerful extroverted manner, whereas I am so taciturn you might even miss that I was there. Jang once said, "While teaching literature and poetry, I became skeptical of imagery, I despaired at the uselessness of poetry, and I was astonished by the breakdown of my language. I had a powerful realization that something else was needed but taking even one step back was difficult. I repeated what I knew to be obvious failures. I questioned why it had happened, the path I had taken, and the very existence I had led. I weighed freedom and liberation and withdrawal and solitude. I walked and walked and burned away. There was nothing left." (An excerpt from Jang Seok-won's acceptance speech at the Kim Daljin Literary Award, "To the Foundation of Poetry," *Lyrical Poetics* Summer 2023 Edition.)

Whenever I read Jang Seok-won's writing, I see

him anew. Seeing his playful exuberance overlap with the inner seriousness and intensity that I had first missed; I look at him in all his dimensions. Suddenly, I'm transported back to the late '80s, the early '90s. I reminisce about sitting in basement makgeolli bars in college neighborhoods and remember the faces of my seniors who used to lead us in cries of "revolution and love."

The analysis of Jang's poetry that identified characteristics of his writing; his, "unrestrained indirect discourse, musical collages, unconventional scattering of images, and rapid rhythm," (Lee Chan) remains an important reference point in understanding his work. At some point I began to focus on the "origins" of his work. No one would refute that revolution and love are the origins of Jang Seok-won's poetry, but even now I am amazed at how that influence has reached into the present day.

I am still amazed by these phrases right out of the '80s, written in these lines, "A firebomb flies from left to right / Catapulted by the White Skull Brigade / A precise and persistent severance...There was a platform of labor liberation and driving out American imperialism" ("Superman returns"). Phrases such as firebomb, White Skull Brigade, catapulted, labor liberation, driving out American imperialism, they still have the power to shock and reading these overlapping words sparks a delirium. Thus, when a person discovers the place that they regard passionately as their starting point, their origins, it can cause a strange twitch in the heart. Some may call it an anachronism, but to me it is as welcome as a person who has ardently guarded a light that refuses to go out, in a place that has been abandoned by all,

Jang Seok-won asks the question of what remains after revolution and love have ended, from the perspective of a man who cannot abandon his ideology and from the metaperspective of a man who imagined a burial in the sky, which is illustrated in the stanzas, "From the / Bed / From the / Table / To the moment / The bottle of pills falls // Another face arrives / I melt under / That other face" ("Spring, screaming"). He torments himself with experiments. He rejects, destroys, and observes the self from the outside and examines himself again without end. This is how I interpret, "I slaughter myself" ("Under construction").

It is astonishing that he does not give up. He may fall, he may break, he may be destroyed, but he never abandons his origins, revolution and love. That is why I love Jang Seok-won's poetry.

PRAISE FOR JANG SEOK-WON

Jang Seok-won does not accept compromise or negotiation in his grand design. In that sense, like the title of his poetry collection, he is an Anarchist. For the anarchist who belongs to no system or category, the only action to take is to ceaselessly reject this world that divides all into conservative or liberal, old or young, male or female, adult or child. The anarchist rejects the past, the present, and ultimately even the self. Thus, the poet says, "All I can do, is tremble and utter one word, 'Terrorize.'" (*Dreams, Movement, Speed, and Glide*)

Jeon Byeong-joon, "Portrait of a lonely anarchist—
Jang Seok-won' s poetry collection
Anarchist" *The Boundaries of Literature*
Spring 2006 Edition (Vol. 20) *Moonji* 2005.

Jang Seok-won's poetry is powerful. His voice—expressed in divisiveness—rings out in his poetry. To Jang, poetry is not "figurative thought" it is a space where "lamentations" are born, and it is a "record of a struggle." In intense excitement, he consumes the world, and the world inhales him. His poetry records this process and, like giving in to fever, accepts the chaos of this world, an unconscious liberation.

Lee Seong-hyuk, "The ethics of devolution—
Jang Seok-won' s poetry collection *The Start of Devolution"*
Creation and Criticism, Summer 2012 Edition.

Sasrava and Anasrava is an aesthetic variation on the course of true love, intensely and beautifully come to fruition. Love's pull is delicately, precisely embodied by the unique musicality that characterizes Jang Seok-won's writing. Jang's voice, combined with relatively diverse poetry forms, shines through in his aesthetics and conveys an extraordinary sense of emotion and simultaneously entices readers to draw on their imaginative experiences and leaves his creative mark on them. These moments may transpire out of our desire, our dream, to become one with language and to span the spaces in the poet's unique language. In that regard, the creative capability of this poetry collection deserves widespread recognition. It is decidedly a brilliant achievement that captures the expansive process of Jang Seok-won's poetry.

Yoo Sung-ho, Judges' Commentary,
34th Kim Daljin Literary Award.

Jang Seok-won's fifth poetry collection, *Sasrava and Anasrava*, opens to a deeply expansive lyricism, with the unrestrained insight that we've come to expect from Jang and a poetic thinking that is curious and lively. Beyond the confessional or declarative, beyond poetic speech and metacritical speech, the poetry collection, The Start of Devolution, identifies false hopes that persist eternally. The volume Rhythm pulls the trigger with glimpses of life in disorder, "My poem is a tiger emerging from my lips." *Sasrava and Anasrava* pierces the invisible—language. Out of a fierce pathos, deriving pleasure from pain, it is incredibly human. "Until one poem, one stanza is created in my body."

Lee Seong-mo, Judges' Commentary,
34th Kim Daljin Literary Award.

K-POET
Parting After Parting

Written by Jang Seok-won
Translated by Deborah Kim
Published by ASIA Publishers
Address 445, Hoedong-gil, Paju-si, Gyeonggi-do, Korea
(Seoul Office: 161-1, Seodal-ro, Dongjak-gu, Seoul, Korea)
Email bookasia@hanmail.net

ISBN 979-11-5662-317-5 (set) | 979-11-5662-650-3 (04810)
First published in Korea by ASIA Publishers 2023

This book is published with the support of the Literature Translation Institute of Korea (LTI Korea).

K-픽션 시리즈 | Korean Fiction Series

〈K-픽션〉 시리즈는 한국문학의 젊은 상상력입니다. 최근 발표된 가장 우수하고 흥미로운 작품을 엄선하여 출간하는 〈K-픽션〉은 한국문학의 생생한 현장을 국내외 독자들과 실시간으로 공유하고자 기획되었습니다. 〈바이링궐 에디션 한국 대표 소설〉 시리즈를 통해 검증된 탁월한 번역진이 참여하여 원작의 재미와 품격을 최대한 살린 〈K-픽션〉 시리즈는 매 계절마다 새로운 작품을 선보입니다.

001 버핏과의 저녁 식사-**박민규** Dinner with Buffett-**Park Min-gyu**
002 아르판-**박형서** Arpan-**Park hyoung su**
003 애드벌룬-**손보미** Hot Air Balloon-**Son Bo-mi**
004 나의 클린트 이스트우드-**오한기** My Clint Eastwood-**Oh Han-ki**
005 이베리아의 전갈-**최민우** Dishonored-**Choi Min-woo**
006 양의 미래-**황정은** Kong's Garden-**Hwang Jung-eun**
007 대니-**윤이형** Danny-**Yun I-hyeong**
008 퇴근-**천명관** Homecoming-**Cheon Myeong-kwan**
009 옥화-**금희** Ok-hwa-**Geum Hee**
010 시차-**백수린** Time Difference-**Baik Sou linne**
011 올드 맨 리버-**이장욱** Old Man River-**Lee Jang-wook**
012 권순찬과 착한 사람들-**이기호** Kwon Sun-chan and Nice People-**Lee Ki-ho**
013 알바생 자르기-**장강명** Fired-**Chang Kang-myoung**
014 어디로 가고 싶으신가요-**김애란** Where Would You Like To Go?-**Kim Ae-ran**
015 세상에서 가장 비싼 소설-**김민정** The World's Most Expensive Novel-**Kim Min-jung**
016 체스의 모든 것-**김금희** Everything About Chess-**Kim Keum-hee**
017 할로윈-**정한아** Halloween-**Chung Han-ah**
018 그 여름-**최은영** The Summer-**Choi Eunyoung**
019 어느 피씨주의자의 종생기-**구병모** The Story of P.C.-**Gu Byeong-mo**
020 모르는 영역-**권여선** An Unknown Realm-**Kwon Yeo-sun**
021 4월의 눈-**손원평** April Snow-**Sohn Won-pyung**
022 서우-**강화길** Seo-u-**Kang Hwa-gil**
023 가출-**조남주** Run Away-**Cho Nam-joo**
024 연애의 감정학-**백영옥** How to Break Up Like a Winner-**Baek Young-ok**
025 창모-**우다영** Chang-mo-**Woo Da-young**
026 검은 방-**정지아** The Black Room-**Jeong Ji-a**
027 도쿄의 마야-**장류진** Maya in Tokyo-**Jang Ryu-jin**
028 홀리데이 홈-**편혜영** Holiday Home-**Pyun Hye-young**
029 해피 투게더-**서장원** Happy Together-**Seo Jang-won**
030 골드러시-**서수진** Gold Rush-**Seo Su-jin**
031 당신이 보고 싶어하는 세상-**장강명** The World You Want to See-**Chang Kang-myoung**
032 지난밤 내 꿈에-**정한아** Last Night, In My Dream-**Chung Han-ah**
Special 휴가중인 시체-**김중혁** Corpse on Vacation-**Kim Jung-hyuk**
Special 사파에서-**방현석** Love in Sa Pa-**Bang Hyeon-seok**

Through literature, you

bilingual Edition Modern

ASIA Publishers' carefully selected

Set 1

Division

Industrialization

Women

Set 2

Liberty

Love and Love

Affairs

South and North

Set 3

Seoul

Tradition

Avant-Garde

Set 4

Diaspora

Family

Humor

Search "bilingual edition

can meet the real Korea!

Korean Literature

22 keywords to understand Korean literature

Set 5

- Relationships
- Discovering
- Everyday Life
- Taboo and Desire

Set 6

- Fate
- Aesthetic Priests
- The Naked in the Colony

Set 7

- Colonial Intellectuals Turned "Idiots"
- Traditional Korea's Lost Faces
- Before and After Liberation
- Korea After the Korean War

korean literature"on Amazon!